Sun Tzu

THE ART OF LEADERSHIP

Matt Shlosberg

Hanna Concern Publishing
Cambridge, MA

Matt Shlosberg
Sun Tzu - The Art of Leadership
Copyright ©2010, Matt Shlosberg

Artwork by Izya Shlosberg
Some artwork is courtesy of free clip art collections
All copyrights and trademarks belong to their respective owners
Special thanks to Dr. John Qian for his contribution to this book

Published by Hanna Concern Publishing

Printed in the United States of America

Library of Congress Control Number: 2010904820
ISBN Number: 1451590466
ISBN-13 Number: 9781451590463

Introduction - From The Author

Welcome to the world of Sun Tzu. Everyone heard of this ancient Chinese general. Most have read his Art of War. Academics around the world agree that it's one of the best books on strategy. But The Art of War contains another jewel very few people thought about - The Art of Leadership.

The Art of War has numerous references to things great leaders do, but no one has ever translated them or pointed them out. The purpose of this book is to do just that.

I want to invite you to take a journey in time and see what The Art of Leadership would have looked like if it was written by Sun Tzu himself. This manuscript is written in the same style as The Art of War. While it looks like it applies to the military, it's actually a great guide to leadership in today's world. The book uses metaphors to make it look antique. The word "general" implies "leader" and "soldier" implies "follower".

Enjoy reading it and building your leadership skills. Just remember, leadership is a practice, not a science. You won't become a good leader by reading this book. You will only become a good leader if you practice what it preaches.

Good luck and have fun!

SUN TZU SAID...

THE FIVE ELEMENTS

The Five Elements...9

Choose Your Soldiers 10

Control Performance 11

What Soldiers Want..12

Leaders At All Levels 13

Effectiveness Of Leadership..............................14

The Dynamics of Competency 15

From Soldier To General 16

Interpersonal Skills 17

Why Soldiers Do Things 18

Yin and Yang 19

The Admired General 20

The Chameleon 21

Stages Of Development 22

Vision..23

Coaching 24

Motivation 25

Empowerment 26

Teams 27

THE FIVE COINS

Emotional Intelligence 31

Self-Awareness 32

Self-Regulation..33

Intrinsic Motivation..34

Empathy 35

Social Skill 36

THE MOON

Leading Change 41

Status Quo 42

Chaos 43

The Danger 44

The Bias 45

Delusions of Success 46

Execution Of Soldiers 47

Humans 48

Leading by Example 49

Categorization 50

The Perfect General 51

Negotiation 52

Talking 53

Power 54

籌略

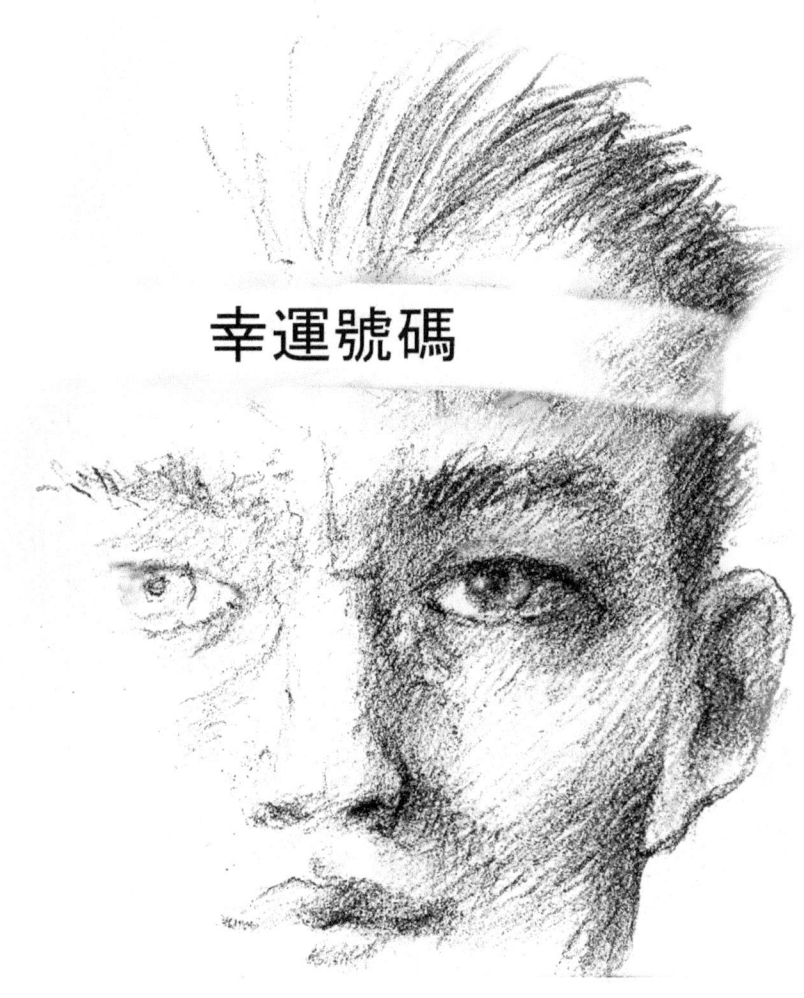

幸運號碼

THE FIVE ELEMENTS

The Five Elements

The Five Elements that make the leader are:
The right people in the right positions,
Mission and vision of the great leader,
Coaching to get to the vision,
Tools needed to execute, and
The leader out of the way of those that do.
Add passion and awareness
And you cannot be beaten!

Choose Your Soldiers

SUN TZU SAID:

Soldiers want to fight, but fighting can be arrogant.
Choose soldiers that fight humbly.
Soldiers may volunteer, but they are not useful.
Politely decline incompetence.
Soldiers may choose not to listen.
Using them is not advantageous.
Soldiers may join you for the wrong reason.
Wrong reasons are worse than incompetence.
Soldiers may do harm if not chosen wisely.
Soldiers may do harm if not placed astutely.
Select your soldiers shrewdly.
Put them in the right positions.

10

Control Performance

Soldiers perform well if chosen wisely,
If they are put in the right positions,
And are led correctly.

If soldier doesn't perform,
See if he's been chosen prudently.
See if he's been placed intelligently,
See if he is being led correctly.

If not chosen prudently, remove him.
If not placed intelligently, move him.
If not led correctly, build or remove the leader.
That's how you control performance.

What Soldiers Want

SUN TZU SAID:

When general leads his soldiers properly,
He gives them want they want.
Soldiers want to perform interesting work.
Soldiers want to be appreciated for what they do.
Soldiers want to be in on things.
Soldiers want to feel secure for their jobs.
Soldiers want good and fair pay.
Soldiers like promotions.
They want to become generals.
Soldiers want good working conditions.
Soldiers want the general to be loyal to them.
Soldiers like tactful discipline.
Soldiers want help them with personal problems.

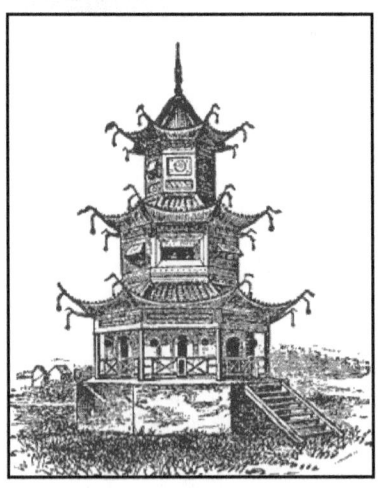

Leaders At All Levels

Soldiers want to become generals.
Soldiers want to feel like generals.
Soldiers want to exercise the Five Elements of
leadership.
You should let them!
You need generals at all levels.
When leaders are placed at all levels,
Your army becomes stronger,
Your people are better prepared to face challenges,
Your people stick with the army,
You have a succession plan,
Your enemy is afraid of you,
Your competitors and friends respect you.

13

Effectiveness Of Leadership

SUN TZU SAID:

Leaders are effective when they are aware.
They should be aware of themselves.
They should be aware of others and
the impact of their actions on others.
They should have situational awareness.

Leaders are effective when they are able.
They should be able to influence others
No matter if they do or don't have authority.
They should be able to make hard decisions,
Even if unacceptable to self.

Leaders are effective when they commit.
They should always do the right thing,
Even if it requires a hard decision.
They take responsibility for their decisions.

If everything goes right, the general simply did his job.
If anything goes wrong, it's his fault!

Effective leaders are aware, able, and committed.
One factor without the other creates problems.

The Dynamics of Competency

SUN TZU SAID:

Leaders are competent and conscious.

If competent but not conscious,
Your effectiveness is lost,
You can master your job but not understand it,
You are only important when things are steady,
You become obsolete when shifts occur.

If conscious but not competent,
You don't know what to do but you are aware,
You are not perfect, but you are close!
Find someone else who is competent,
Find another way to do your job.
Awareness is key.

15

From Soldier To General

SUN TZU SAID:

Soldiers want to become generals.
Soldiers want to feel like generals.
But soldiers must change to become generals.

Soldiers fight, generals command.
As soldiers grow, they fight less.
As soldiers grow, they command more.
As soldiers grow, they focus on resources.
But both soldiers and generals
communicate the same way.
The demand for interpersonal skills never changes.

16

Interpersonal Skills

Interpersonal skills aren't about talking.
Interpersonal skills call for results.

Results occur if you can convince others of your ideas,
If you are open to talk, if you can receive feedback,
If you can talk to anyone, even the general,
If you can listen, if you know when to talk,
If you can be clear, if you talk with passion,
If you are trusted, if you promote innovation,
If you coach, but do so wisely,
If you can face problems and make changes,
If you are reliable, if time is your tool,
If you seek input, influence others,
If you have courage, make hard decisions,
Resolve any conflict, think win-win situation,
Create productive soldiers, take risks appropriately,
Critically reflect, take responsibility,
Communicate your dream.

17

Why Soldiers Do Things

SUN TZU SAID:

Coercion is effective!
Soldiers execute when you force them.
But coercion shows your weakness, -
Soldiers view you as scared and incompetent.
If you force them, they will join your enemy.
Don't force them.

Money is great, but money is evil.
Soldiers want money if they don't have it.
Soldiers do things for money, if they want money.
If they don't want money, they won't be effective.
Don't promise them money to work for you.

People do well when they are motivated.
Do motivate people and you will succeed.
Set motivation as an expectation.

People want to belong. People want to care.
People want to believe in what they do.
Give them what they want and you will succeed.
Set identification as an expectation.

Ownership goes farther than everything else.
Do build owners and you will succeed.

Yin and Yang

The task you assign to your solders is Yin.
The relationship you have with soldiers is Yang.
It's hard to balance the two.

If you force Yin without Yang,
They will hate you but they will do as you say.

If you force Yang without Yin,
They will love you but won't do as you say.

If you balance Yin and Yang,
They will love you and do as you say.

Leaders know how to balance Yin and Yang.
The world of effective leadership lies
In the place where Yin and Yang are combined.

Balancing Yin and Yang is
The Art of Leadership.

The Admired General

Generals can lead but not be admired.
To be admired, the general must wear seven rings.

The blue ring of honesty can be worn by those
Who possess the highest level of integrity.
The green ring of vision can be worn by those
Who are always forward looking.
The red ring of passion can be worn by those
Who inspire, have positive attitude, and energy.
The black ring of competence can be worn by those
Who possess great judgment and technical skills.
The white ring of credibility can be worn by those
Who possess the first four rings.
The golden ring of fairness can be worn by those
Who treat their soldiers fairly.
The yellow ring of support can be worn by those
Who support followers.

I once met a general who wore all seven rings.
He was highly admired.
Not many generals have all seven,
But finding these rings is easy.

The Chameleon

SUN TZU SAID:

Chameleons are great leaders.
They change with situation they are in.
They know their color doesn't always protect them.
They are flexible. They evaluate each situation.
There's no one best way to lead.
Great generals are chameleons.
Their actions depend on the situation.

Stages Of Development

When you have Novice soldiers,
Don't expect anything from them.
Just give them a lot of direction.

When you have Apprentice soldiers,
Expect some, but teach them!
Give them some direction.
Give them a lot of feedback.

When you have Journeyman soldiers,
Expect a lot, but not mastery.
Give them some direction.
Give them a lot of feedback.

When soldiers become Masters,
Leave them alone.
They don't need your direction.
They don't need your feedback.

Help your soldiers move between stages.
From Novice to Apprentice and then to Journeyman.
Most soldiers will remain as Journeyman.
Move the best ones to the Mastery stage.

Vision

SUN TZU SAID:

You must have a dream.
You must tell your soldiers about your dream.
You must explain the meaning of your dream.
Your dream must make sense.
Your dream must be complete.
Your dream must rethink the possibilities.
You must sell your dream to your soldiers.
You can't force your dream onto others.

If soldiers like your dream,
It will become their own dream.
It will become everyone's vision.
It will get you places.

If soldiers don't like your dream,
It will remain a dream of your own.

Coaching

Coaching is an argument.
People have positions.
When people have positions, no one wins.
When people have positions, coaching is worthless.

To win an argument, destroy positions,
Create a common problem,
Solve it together.
You can't win an argument if the other party loses.
Let the other party win and you will win too.

To destroy positions, ask questions.
Maybe your position is wrong?
Find a common goal.
Achieve the goal together.

This is what effective coaching is about.

Motivation

Soldiers do better when motivated.
Personality plays a role, but it can't be controlled.
They should like their jobs.
You should meet their needs.
You should give them rewards.
You should treat them fairly.
You should give them interesting work.
You should help them become self confident.
You should be good to them.
You should promote them.
You should give them good working conditions.
They should like other soldiers.

You should set expectations and goals.
They must be clear, achievable, challenging,
Very specific, measurable, accepted, agreed.
You should provide soldiers with feedback.
You should hold soldiers individually accountable.

Empowerment

Generals empower their soldiers.
Good soldiers are empowered.
Great soldiers own the army.

First soldiers wait to be told.
Then soldiers ask for permission.
Then soldiers make recommendations.
Then soldiers take action and report to the general.
Then soldiers take action and never report.
These soldiers are owners.

If your soldiers take action and never report,
If they make good decisions while doing so,
If you are happy with results,
You've achieved the highest level of empowerment.

If your soldiers don't want to get empowered,
It's okay. Let them be.
Some soldiers want to stay where they are.

26

Teams

SUN TZU SAID:

Soldiers work in teams. But teams don't perform well.
I once saw a team that performed skillfully.
Team members inquired, but not advocated.
They used devil's advocates, but they were respectful.
They were very diverse.
They learned from one another.
They were open to each other's opinions.
They modified their own opinions.
They planned for how they can reach decisions.
Everyone was involved. All were treated equally.
They didn't allow social loafing.
People were aligned to purpose.
People were aligned to task.
They shared responsibility.
They had an open, candid talk,
They were innovative.
I heard no dominant voices.

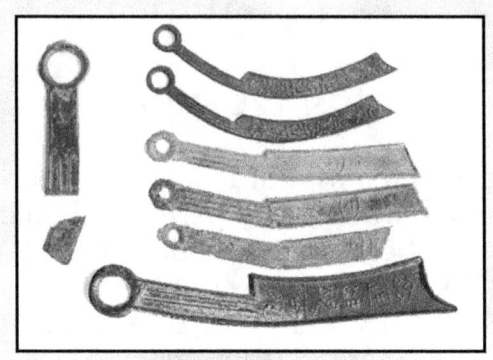

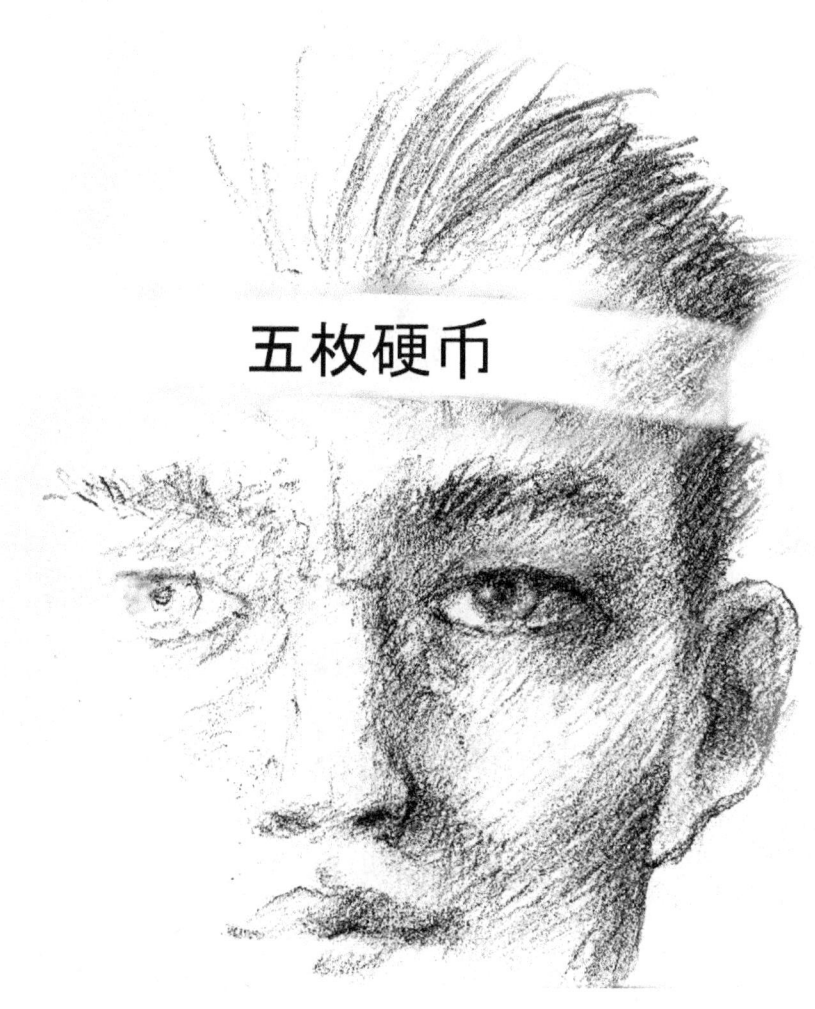

五枚硬币

THE FIVE COINS

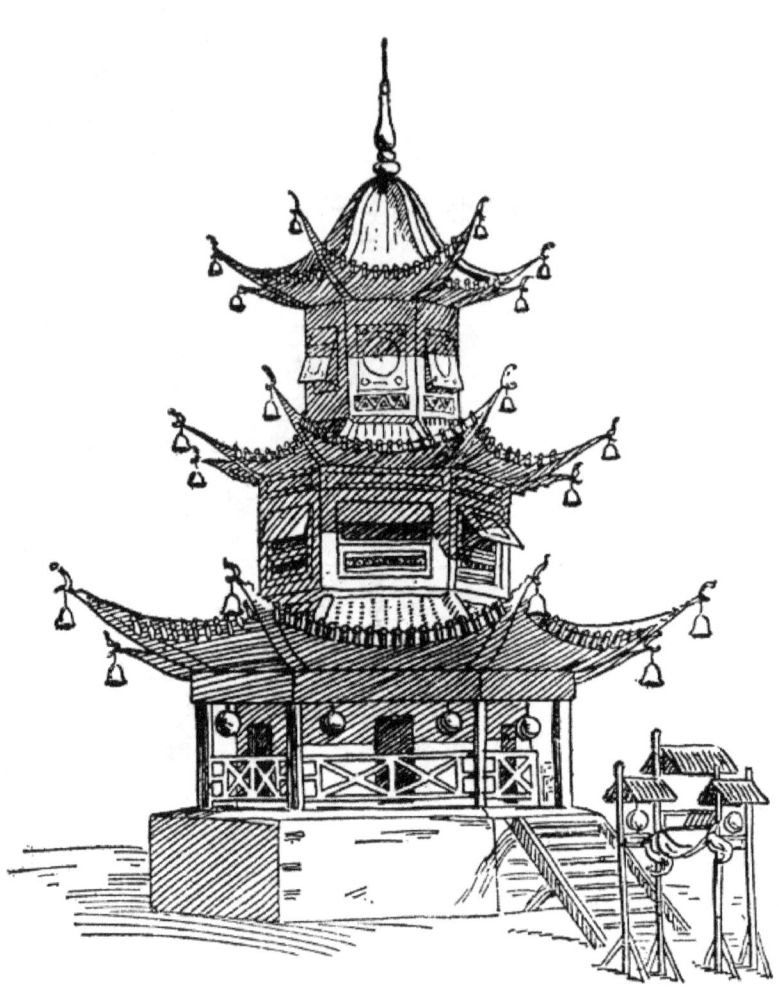

Emotional Intelligence

SUN TZU SAID:

I once met a general who had five coins.
He had a silver coin of self-awareness,
A gold coin of self-regulation,
A copper coin of intrinsic motivation,
A glass coin of empathy,
And a platinum coin of social skill.

He showed his coins to everyone around him.
His soldiers loved him.
Enemies were afraid of him.
Other generals respected him.
His coins possessed the power
Of emotional intelligence.

This power can be gained by anyone!
Just find these coins. It's not hard!
But these coins only give you full power
When they are all together.

Self-Awareness

SUN TZU SAID:

The coin of self-awareness is powerful!
It lets you know thyself.
It lets you understand your own emotions.
It opens your eyes to your own strengths.
It helps you understand your weaknesses.
It forces you to be honest with yourself.

This coin is tough to find if you are weak.
This coin is easy to find if you are strong.

Self-Regulation

SUN TZU SAID:

The coin of self-regulation is worth more than gold.
But it's worthless without the coin of self-awareness.

The power to manage your feelings,
The power to control your impulses,
The power to think before acting,
The power of self-discipline,
All can be given to you
If you obtain this coin.

Anyone can find this coin,
But not everyone searches for it.

Look and you will find.

Intrinsic Motivation

SUN TZU SAID:

Great generals have great personality.
They feel driven to achieve beyond expectations.
They pursue goals with energy and persistence.
They don't care about money.

They achieve because they possess the copper coin.
The copper coin of intrinsic motivation.

This coin is hard to find.
But one can find it if he is self driven.

34

Empathy

SUN TZU SAID:

The coin of empathy is made out of glass.
You can see through glass.
You can see feelings of other people.
You can consider their feelings when making decisions.
You can understand the emotional make up of others.
You can treat people according to their emotions.
You can show respect for perspectives of others.
You can be aware of others.

Look through the coin,
Look for the coin.
It gives you great power.

35

Social Skill

The platinum coin of social skill is supreme.
It moves people in the right direction.
It manages your relationships.
It builds networks of people.
It builds common ground and bond.
It persuades others.
It builds and leads teams.

Find this coin!
You won't feel sorry!

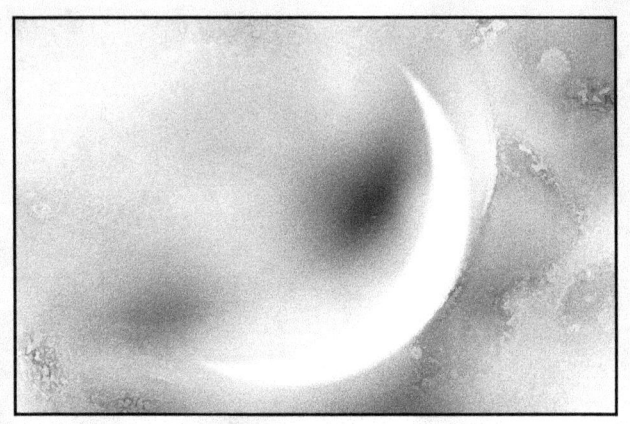

籌略

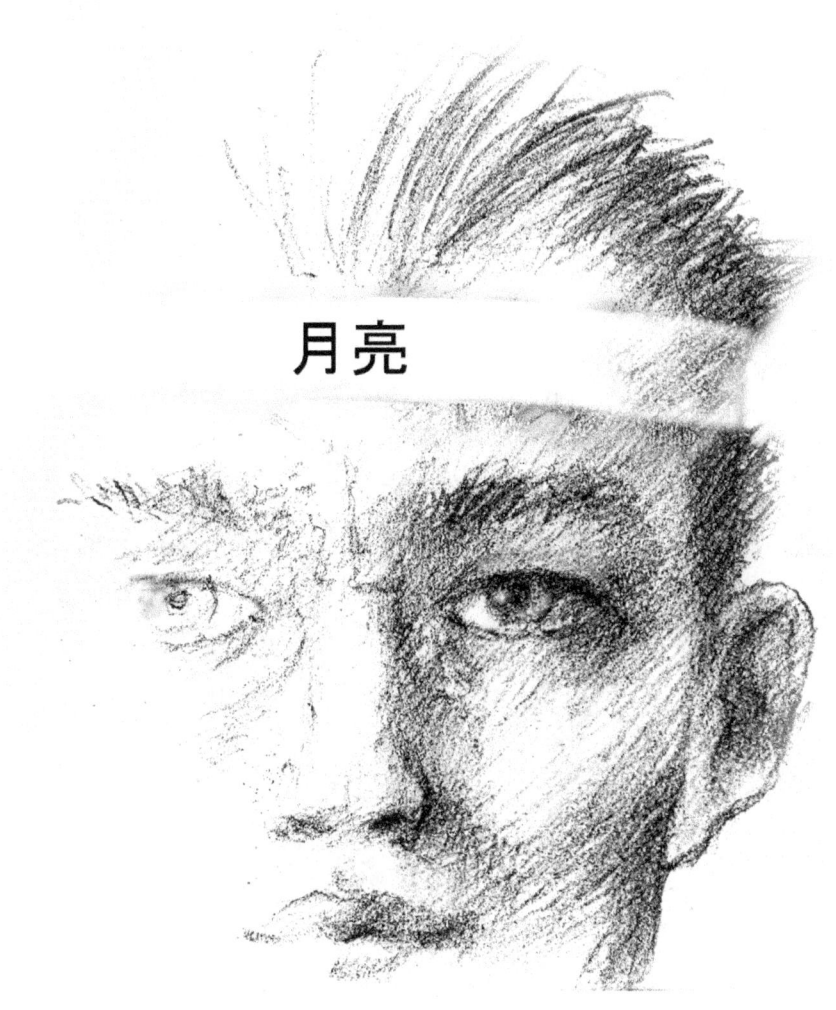

月亮

THE MOON

Leading Change

SUN TZU SAID:

Change is difficult. Soldiers resist.
Sell to the soldiers. Don't force change.
If they buy it, you have power.
If they don't buy it. Remove them.

To bring change, unfreeze the old.
Don't reinforce it.

Communicate the new.
Create a sense of identification with the new.
Give soldiers a voice. Change attitudes.
Ask, don't tell. Sell. Don't force.
Respect.
Explain the reasons. Soldiers want to know.
Explain how you will achieve change.
Enforce the new.

Freeze the new.

Status Quo

SUN TZU SAID:

Leaders challenge status quo

Chaos

SUN TZU SAID:

The world is tough. The world is diverse.
There are many wise men, but none are wise.
There's abundance. There's shortage.
People think they know what they want.
But people don't know what they want.

Soldiers like structure. Soldiers like to know.
But the world has no structure. They can't know.
It's okay for soldiers to see structure.
It's okay for them to know.
But the general shouldn't see structure.
The general should build structure
In the minds of soldiers,
Not in his own!

The general lives in the world of chaos.
He understands it. He respects it.
He uses it to build structures for others.
He uses it to control his soldiers.

The Danger

Teams can be good. Teams can be bad.
Teams can solve problems better than one person.
One person can solve problems better than teams.

Group think destroys brilliant minds.
Brilliant minds need other brilliant minds.

Great people think alike,
But it's a problem!

44

The Bias

SUN TZU SAID:

When soldiers are born, they have instincts.
Then they gain knowledge, but knowledge isn't true.
Knowledge comes from other soldiers.

Soldiers have opinions.
If knowledge is based on opinions,
Then all knowledge is biased.
Knowledge is based on opinions.

In two thousand years
People will invent mechanic horses.
They will fly mechanic birds.
They will have light with no fire.
They will talk to each other without couriers.
They will have different opinions.
They will have different knowledge.

The less we know, the more we think we know.
The more we know, the more biased we are.
Be careful! Remove biases!

Delusions of Success

People are delusional.
Soldiers are delusional.
Generals are delusional.

But be careful!
Delusion of success is just a dream.
Wishful thinking is not strategy.
Neglect of your enemy can destroy you.
Optimism without reason is just an ego.

Be optimistic, but don't fall into this trap!
Dreaming is good, but do have a plan!
What happens if you are wrong?

Execution Of Soldiers

No one is perfect! Even the general!
If you are ready to execute a soldier,
Think of the Five Elements.
Is he the right person? Is he in the right position?
Did you communicate a vision?
Did you give him a mission?
Did you give him the tools?
Did you coach him?
Did you get out of his way?

Is your soldier motivated?
Does he understand the task?
Does he understand the purpose?
Does he understand what you expect?
Did he have an opportunity to prove himself?
Was he in the environment allowing him to perform?

If you said no, execute yourself. It's your mistake!
If you said yes, then what went wrong?
Are you self-aware?
Did you make a mistake?

Humans

SUN TZU SAID:

Soldiers are humans. Generals are humans.

Humans are lazy when making decisions.
Humans take shortcuts.
Humans categorize. Humans form opinions.
They form first impressions.
Humans do what worked before.
Humans change believes to those surrounding them.
Humans follow dominant voices.
Humans can be framed. They escalate commitments.
Humans take risks in teams but not alone.

Soldiers are humans.

Soldiers behave with others
The way their general behaves with them.

Leading by Example

SUN TZU SAID:

The general tells his troops what to do.
The troops listen and obey.
If his troops believe in his orders, they are successful.
If his troops don't believe in his orders,
There's a risk of failure.

If the general doesn't lead by example,
His troops don't believe in his orders.
The general isn't any different from his troops.
The general is a soldier.
The general applies his own rules to himself.

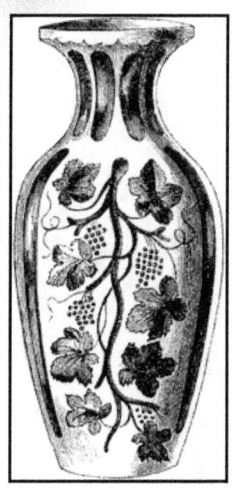

Categorization

SUN TZU SAID:

There's black and white,
Yin and Yang.
There are always two sides of the story.
Great generals always look at both sides.
They remember,
Great geniuses look dumb.

The Perfect General

SUN TZU SAID:

I once met the perfect general.
He knew it all. He did it all.
He showed the best example of leadership.
He didn't have to improve.
He didn't want to improve.
He didn't need to improve.
He was the only perfect general in the world.

Then I woke up.

Negotiation

SUN TZU SAID:

Negotiating with your enemy is advantageous.
If you win the negotiation, you both lost.
If your enemy won the negotiation, you both lost.
If you both win the negotiation, you both win.
Negotiation can't have a single winner.

To have two winners,
Don't press your agenda.
Share your ideals, ask your enemies for ideals.
Then solve the problem together.

52

Talking

SUN TZU SAID:

Talking is an art.
Asking questions is an art.
Be wise when you talk.
Be wise when you ask.

Wise men know what to say.
Wise men know when to say it.
Wise men know when to listen.

Silence is the best language.
It carries more power than talking.

Power

SUN TZU SAID:

Generals are powerful.
The emperor is powerful.
The God is powerful.
Arrows are powerful.
Soldiers are powerful.

Generals have authority.
The emperor has authority.
The God has authority.
Arrows act with authority.
Soldiers act with authority.

All are powerful if they have authority.
But the most powerful of all
Are generals that have power without authority.

54

籌略

THE ART OF
LEADERSHIP

www.ingramcontent.com/pod-product-compliance
Lightning Source LLC
Chambersburg PA
CBHW051248170526
45165CB00004B/1624